AN
EASY-READ
FACT
BOOK

Arms and Armor

77556

F. Wilkinson

Franklin Watts

London   New York   Toronto   Sydney

© 1984 Franklin Watts Ltd

First published in Great Britain
   1984 by
Franklin Watts Ltd
12a Golden Square
London W1

First published in the USA by
Franklin Watts Inc.
387 Park Avenue South
New York
N.Y. 10016

UK ISBN: 0 86313 166 2
US ISBN: 0-531-03773-3
Library of Congress Catalog Card
   Number: 83-51439

Designed by
Jim Marks

Edited by
Judith Maxwell

Illustrated by
Jim Marks
Jeff Burn
John James/Temple Art

Photographs supplied by
Paul Forrester
The Photographers' Library
The Bridgeman Art Library
Robert Harding

Printed in Great Britain by
   Cambus Litho, East Kilbride

Arms and Armor

Contents

The first weapons

Early people used stones and sticks to kill animals and to fight one another. Stone Age hunters found that a stone called flint could be split into pieces with sharp edges. They made flint arrow heads, small axes and knives.

About 5,000 years ago, people found out how to make bronze. This metal could be melted, poured into a mold and allowed to cool. Metal workers, or smiths, made bronze axes, spear heads, daggers and swords. Bronze weapons were much better than flint and did not break so easily.

An even stronger metal, iron, was discovered about 3,000 years ago. Iron weapons stayed sharper than bronze and were much tougher.

At this time, there were two main kinds of weapon – throwing weapons, such as spears, and hitting weapons, such as swords. Some warriors wore armor to protect their bodies.

△Flint axe (left) and arrow heads of the Stone Age. The arrow-heads were pushed into slits in wooden shafts and tied in place.

▷Smiths melted down bronze and poured it into molds. When it was hard, they polished and sharpened the finished weapons.

4

▷A bronze axe (left) and a spear head. Bronze heads were also often tied on to wooden shafts.

Ancient warfare

Early soldiers fought only in small groups and on foot. The first armies were those of Egypt and Assyria.

The Egyptians fought in chariots, which were light, two-wheeled carts pulled by two horses. Each chariot carried two men. One man controlled the horses. The second man was the fighter. As the chariot charged into the enemy soldiers, he threw spears or loosed arrows from his bow. Some soldiers wore armor made of small metal plates laced together.

There were also many foot soldiers in the Egyptian army. A foot soldier did not wear armor. He carried a spear, and a wooden shield covered with leather. Some foot soldiers fought with clubs called maces. The mace had a wooden handle and a stone head. Others carried swords and daggers made of bronze or iron. These were sometimes decorated with silver.

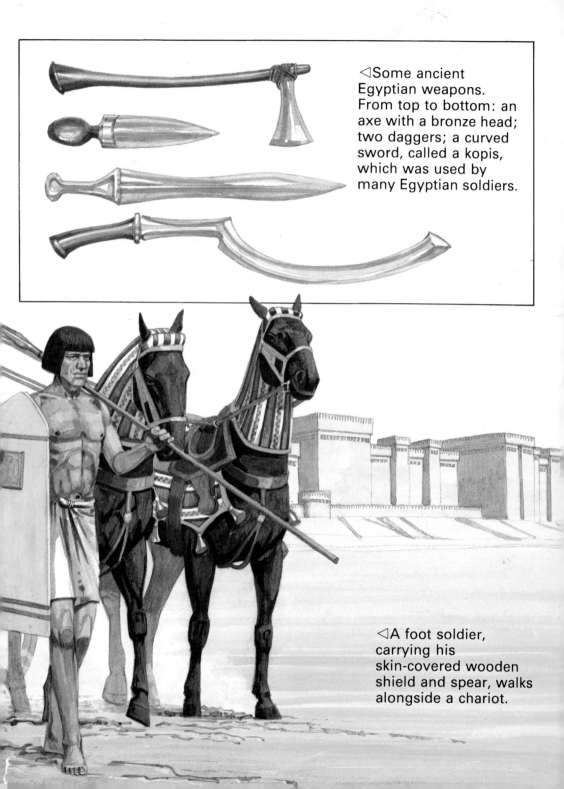

◁Some ancient
Egyptian weapons.
From top to bottom: an
axe with a bronze head;
two daggers; a curved
sword, called a kopis,
which was used by
many Egyptian soldiers.

◁A foot soldier,
carrying his
skin-covered wooden
shield and spear, walks
alongside a chariot.

Greek and Roman soldiers

The soldiers of Greece and Rome were the best-armed and most skilful warriors in the ancient world. Greek soldiers were known as hoplites. They wore bronze helmets with crests of horse hair or feathers. The Greeks wore bronze body armor and carried large, round shields.

A Roman soldier was called a legionary. He wore a plain iron helmet with a neck guard. Roman armor was made of metal plates. It could be folded up for carrying on the march.

▷A hoplite (left) carried a short sword and a long spear. The legionary (right) was armed with a short, broad sword called a gladius. His curved wooden shield was strengthened with pieces of iron to turn aside spears or swords.

▽ **1** and **2** Greek hoplites' swords.
3 A Roman gladius.
4 A Greek spear head.
5 Head of a Roman throwing spear.

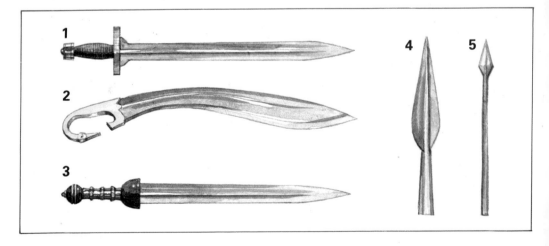

9

Viking warriors

The Vikings of Scandinavia were daring sailors and good fighters. About 1,000 years ago, they crossed the seas in their longships to trade or to raid other lands.

The Vikings wore helmets made of iron with special guards to protect the face. Their body armor was a coat of mail, made from lots of small iron rings joined together.

During battle, the Vikings carried round wooden shields, made stronger with iron bars. When at sea, the Vikings hung their shields along the sides of their longships.

▷Vikings landing from a longship for a raid. A favorite Viking weapon was the long-handled axe. This was held in both hands. Viking swords had straight blades and were used to slash rather than stab.

Arming a knight

For many centuries, the knight was the most heavily armed warrior. He fought on horseback and wore armor. A knight needed a servant or squire to help him into his armor.

First he put on a padded tunic with patches of mail sewn on. He sometimes also wore a mail skirt. Then armor for the feet and legs was fastened in place. Next came the armor for the body — the breast and back plates — and the arm pieces. Finally, the knight put on his gloves, called gauntlets, and helmet.

Armor was not as heavy as it looks, and a fully armored knight could move about quite easily. However, it was hot and stuffy inside the armor.

The knight rode a big, powerful horse. A group of knights charging into the enemy was hard to stop. Their weapons were swords, maces and long spears called lances.

▷A knight in his arming doublet with his squire helping him into the armor. When all the pieces were in place, the squire would check that all the straps and laces were fastened securely. He would also make sure that the knight could move easily in his armor.

Archers

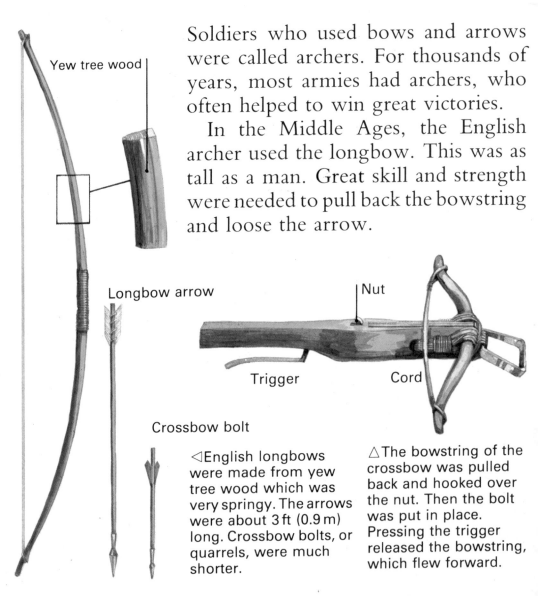

Yew tree wood

Soldiers who used bows and arrows were called archers. For thousands of years, most armies had archers, who often helped to win great victories.

In the Middle Ages, the English archer used the longbow. This was as tall as a man. Great skill and strength were needed to pull back the bowstring and loose the arrow.

Longbow arrow

Nut

Trigger

Cord

Crossbow bolt

◁English longbows were made from yew tree wood which was very springy. The arrows were about 3 ft (0.9 m) long. Crossbow bolts, or quarrels, were much shorter.

△The bowstring of the crossbow was pulled back and hooked over the nut. Then the bolt was put in place. Pressing the trigger released the bowstring, which flew forward.

▽ Pulling back the bowstring of the crossbow took quite a long time. This archer has a hook on his belt to help him pull back the cord.

The crossbow was a different kind of bow. It was a very powerful weapon, but it took longer to load than the longbow. The crossbow fired short arrows called bolts or quarrels.

△ The longbow archer could loose many more arrows more quickly than the crossbowman.

Swords and daggers

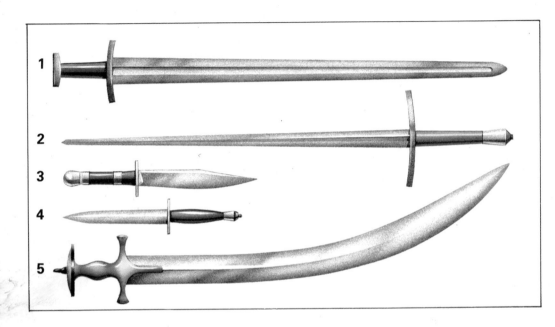

△**1** A knight's war sword.
2 This sword has a stiff, thin blade and was used to stab.
3 A Bowie knife, named after the American frontiersman, James Bowie.
4 World War II commando knife.
5 An Indian sword, the talwar.

Men often carried daggers in sheaths at their belts, for they were used as tools as well as weapons. In the 1600s, men sometimes fought with a sword in one hand and a dagger in the other. The dagger was used to catch the enemy's sword blade.

Large knives were used for hunting. A famous one, called the Bowie knife, had a double cutting edge at the tip.

The sword was a popular weapon, and there were many kinds. Some were so big they were held in both hands. The rapier was much thinner and lighter. Some swords had straight blades designed to stab. Others were curved and were better for cutting. Swords are no longer used in war. People still enjoy the sport of fencing. They use swords without points.

△In the Wild West, quarrels were sometimes settled by a duel fought with Bowie knives. Each fighter held one end of a scarf between his teeth. He could not let go of the scarf until the duel was finished.

The first guns

△ Artillery was used a great deal during the Civil War (1861–5). This cannon is behind a wall of earth to protect the gunners from enemy fire. The cannon balls are stacked in piles ready for use.

The first guns in Europe were made in the 1300s. Early cannons were small and fired arrows. Later ones fired solid balls of stone or iron. Gunpowder was poured down the barrel, and a ball was rammed down on top. The gun was fired by setting light to the powder through a small touch hole at the closed end, or breech, of the gun.

At first, cannons were clumsy. Later they were mounted on wheels so that they could be moved easily around the battlefield. They fired shells. Some exploding shells were filled with bullets which were showered over a wide area.

Today's artillery can hit targets many miles away.

△ This modern tank protects troops against attack from the air. It can fire automatically at targets too far away for the gunners to see.

Pistols

▽ A duel was a fight between two men who had quarreled. They often used an identical pair of pistols. These dueling pistols were kept together in a wooden case. Each pistol fired just one shot.

Pistols are small enough to be used with just one hand. The first ones were made during the 1500s. Some of these were richly decorated. In the 1700s and 1800s, matching pairs of pistols were made specially for use in duels.

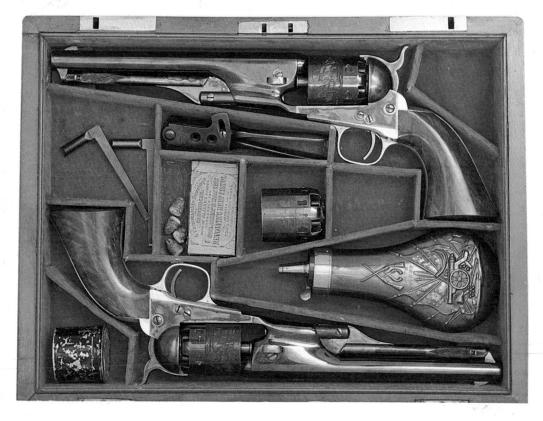

Most early handguns could only be loaded with one shot. In 1836 an American gunmaker, Samuel Colt, designed a revolver which could be loaded with five or six shots. The Colt had a cap to fire the gunpowder. Later guns used cartridges – cases containing cap, powder and ball.

Modern pistols can be loaded with up to fifteen cartridges. They are put in a case called a magazine.

△ A pair of six-shot Colt revolvers in a wooden case. The case also contains a flask of gunpowder, a mold for making bullets, some caps and a spare cylinder.

21

Rifles

△ Loading a musket. First, powder was poured down the barrel. Then a wad and a bullet were pushed down using a ramrod.

The inside of an early gun barrel was a smooth tube. The bullet did not fit very tightly inside. When the gun was fired, the bullet wobbled as it moved along the barrel. This made it difficult to hit the target.

Gunmakers found that the answer to this problem was to cut spiral grooves on the inside of the barrel. As the bullet moved along the barrel these grooves, called rifling, made it spin. The spin made the bullet fly straight and true.

It was not easy to cut rifling, and rifled guns were rare until the 1700s. The American long rifles of the 1700s, called Kentucky or Pennsylvania rifles, were famous for their fine shooting. Today, machines can cut rifling easily. Most modern guns have rifled barrels and are very accurate. Shotguns still have smooth barrels, because they fire a cluster of small pellets, called shot, and not single bullets.

△ A Winchester lever-action rifle.

▽ With the invention of the metal cartridge, it became easy to make repeating guns. These can be fired a number of times before being reloaded. Each cartridge is taken from the magazine in turn and fed into the breech. This may be done by a lever which moves up and down or by a bolt which moves back and forth.

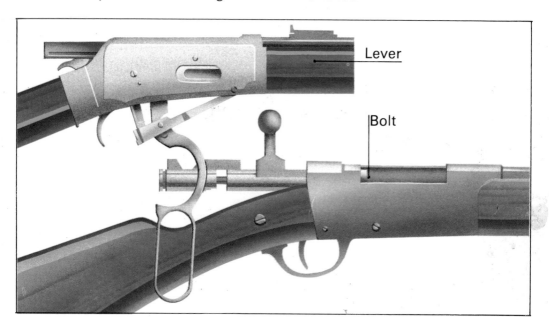

Lever

Bolt

Weapons today

Today, soldiers are armed with fast-firing submachine guns or self-loading rifles. The rifle may be fitted with a long knife, called a bayonet. It may also have a special sight, which enables a soldier to see and hit a target even in darkness.

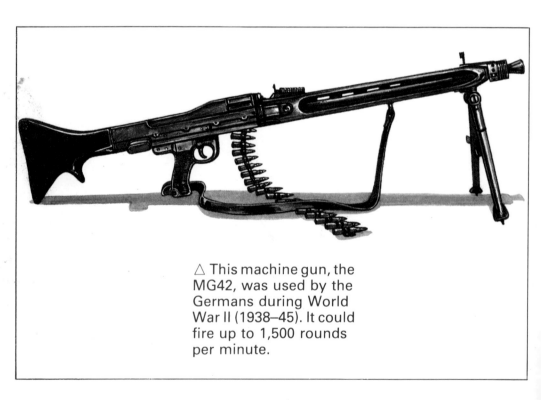

△ This machine gun, the MG42, was used by the Germans during World War II (1938–45). It could fire up to 1,500 rounds per minute.

These guns will go on firing for as long as the trigger is pressed, or until they run out of cartridges. The cartridges are fed in from a magazine. As each cartridge is fired, gas is produced. Some of this gas is used to drive the moving parts which fire the next cartridge.

△ Two AK47 submachine guns. This gun is simple to use, and is strong enough to work under the worst conditions. It is used by many soldiers around the world.

The modern soldier

The modern soldier can use many weapons besides fast-firing guns. He may throw small bombs, called grenades. He can attack more distant targets using small guided missiles.

Soldiers sometimes have to deal with angry crowds. Then they may use special guns which fire plastic or rubber bullets. These are meant to frighten people rather than to kill.

Many soldiers wear plastic helmets, and special jackets that can stop bullets fired from handguns.

▷ Modern armor is often made of plastic, which is lighter but stronger than iron or steel. The special wadding in this flak jacket will stop the bullets from most pistols and revolvers. Extra plates are needed to keep out rifle bullets.

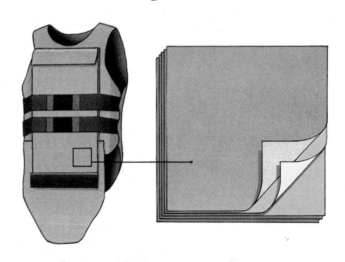

◁ Many modern soldiers wear some kind of body armor. This protects them from small bullets, and from splinters of bombs or shells. The soldier's self-loading rifle can fire a single shot or go on firing for as long as the trigger is pressed.

27

Strange weapons

Many strange weapons have been used in different parts of the world. The kris from Malaya is a knife with a wavy, snake-like blade. The chakram of northern India was a flat steel ring with a sharp edge. It was whirled round to send it spinning through the air.

Some weapons were made to look harmless. Others were designed to be hidden. The Indian tiger claws had several curved blades fitted to a short bar, which was hidden in the hand.

▽ This two-bladed penknife is also a pistol. The trigger folds up when not in use. The weapon also contains a mold for making bullets.

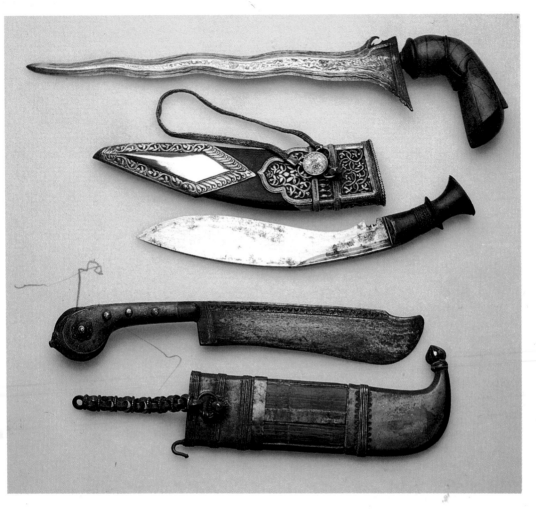

Weapons often had more than one use. For example, hunters carried swords which had a pistol fitted to the blade. If they were attacked, the hunters had two ways of defending themselves. There were also whips which had a pistol hidden in the grip.

△ Top: the wavy bladed kris from Malaya. Middle: the kukri, used by the famous Gurkha soldiers of Nepal. Bottom: a pichangatti from India.

Glossary

Here is a list of some of the technical words used in this book.

Artillery
Large guns that can fire shells over long distances.

Bayonet
A knife fastened to the barrel of a gun.

Cartridge
Early guns were loaded by pouring loose gunpowder down the barrel. Then the bullet was pushed in. Later the gunpowder was packed in small paper tubes called cartridges. Then both bullet and powder were put in the same cartridge. Modern cartridges are made of metal.

Doublet
A coat worn by a knight beneath his armor. Patches of mail were often sewn on parts of the doublet not covered by armor.

Fencing
A way of using a sword both to attack and to defend. Fencing became very popular in the 1500s, and is still enjoyed as a sport today.

Gauntlet
A glove used in medieval times. It was usually covered with mail or armor.

Gunpowder
A mixture of three chemicals first used by the Chinese nearly 1,000 years ago. When touched by fire, it explodes with a loud roar and a cloud of smoke. It is sometimes called black powder.

Magazine
A store for gunpowder, or a part of a gun which holds a number of cartridges.

Shell
A large cartridge used by artillery. Some shells can carry gas or make smoke. They may have special heads that explode when they hit the target.

Shotgun
A gun with a smooth barrel and no rifling. It fires cartridges loaded with a number of small lead balls, or shot.

Smith
A person who works with metal.

Stone Age
The time during which people made tools and weapons from a kind of stone known as flint. The Stone Age ended when people learned how to use metals.

▷ The Armalite rifle fires small, powerful bullets. It can be used to fire either a single shot or up to 800 rounds a minute.

Arms and armor facts

Here are some interesting facts about arms and armor.

For many years, the best arms and armor were made in Italy and Germany.

The best British armor was made in a workshop set up by King Henry VIII at Greenwich, near London.

In 1857, the firm of Smith and Wesson made the first modern type of revolver, loaded with metal cartridges. This firm still makes revolvers.

A modern machine gun can fire nearly 1,000 shots a minute.

The Japanese made the world's best swords. A Japanese warrior, called a samurai, wore armor which was very different from that made in Europe. He carried two swords, one long and one short.

In the Tower of London there is a cannon, made in 1464, which could fire a ball over 24 ins (63 cm) in diameter a distance of 1 mile (1.6 km).

Gurkhas are famous soldiers from Nepal. Every Gurkha carries a curved knife called a kukri.

During World War I (1914–18), British soldiers fired their rifles so quickly that the Germans thought they were using machine guns.

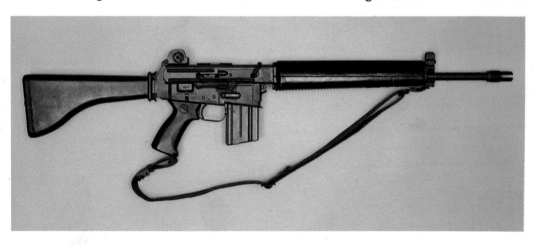

31

Index